Neil Armstrong: 130 Fascinating Facts For Kids

Rod Weston

This book is just one of a series of "Fascinating Facts For Kids" books. For more fascinating facts about people, history, animals and much more please visit:

www.fascinatingfactsforkids.com

Contents

Early Life

1. Neil Alden Armstrong was born just after midnight on August 5, 1930, in his grandparents' Ohio farmhouse. He was the first child of Stephen and Viola Armstrong.

2. When Neil was three years old his sister, June, was born and two years later a younger brother, Dean, became a new addition to the Armstrong family.

3. Neil's father worked for the state government of Ohio, and his job meant that the family had to move house regularly. In the first thirteen years of Neil's life, the Armstrongs moved sixteen times before eventually settling in the small Ohio town of Wapakoneta.

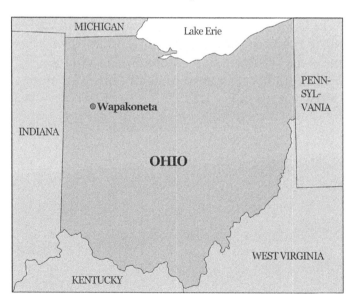

4. Neil was a well-behaved, serious child who loved reading and learning. By the end of his first year at school he had read over 100 books!

5. When Neil was very young he persuaded his mother to buy him a twenty-cent toy airplane, and he became fascinated with flying. This fascination became even stronger when his father took him to an air show in Cleveland, Ohio.

6. Neil dreamed about flying in an airplane, and his dream came true just before his sixth birthday. The local airport was offering cheap plane rides, so Neil's father paid for the two of them to make their first trip in an airplane.

7. The machine that first took Neil into the air was a Ford Trimotor, which was nicknamed the "Tin Goose." It flew noisily through the air at more than 100 miles per hour (160 kph) with passengers sitting in scratchy wicker chairs. Neil's father was scared to death, but Neil loved every second of the trip!

A Ford Trimotor

8. Neil loved building balsa wood model planes that he hung from the ceiling of his bedroom. His ambition was to become an aircraft designer, and decided he should learn to fly in order to get a better understanding of how airplanes work.

Learning to Fly

9. Neil's parents had always insisted that their children pay for their hobbies and interests with their own money, and Neil took on a variety of jobs to pay for his airplane-modeling materials, including mowing the lawn of a cemetery and working in a doughnut factory.

10. As well as a passion for airplanes, Neil also had a love of music. His work at the doughnut factory earned him enough money to buy a baritone horn and join the school band.

11. Flying tuition at the local airfield cost nine dollars an hour (over $100 in today's money) and to pay for the course of lessons Neil took on a job at a drugstore which paid forty cents an hour. He had to work for more than twenty-two hours to pay for one flying lesson!

12. Neil worked hard at the drugstore and eventually saved enough money for flying lessons. He learned to fly during the summer of 1946, and on August 5, which was his sixteenth birthday, he got the best present he could wish for - his pilot's licence. He had learned to fly before he could drive a car!

College & the Navy

13. With a pilot's licence in his possession, Neil decided that when he finished high school he would like to go to college to study aircraft engineering. A college education would be expensive, but Neil had heard about a scholarship program that would provide financial assistance.

14. The scholarship, known as the "Holloway Plan," was offered by the US Naval Aviation College Program. The program would pay for four years of college education, and in return for the scholarship money, Neil would have to serve three years in the Navy. Neil was happy with this arrangement as there were lots of pilots in the Navy and he would be able to fly airplanes!

15. After passing the Holloway Plan qualifying test, Neil was told that he could select a college of his choice. He chose Purdue University, 150 miles (240 km) away in West Lafayette, Indiana, because of its highly respected engineering program.

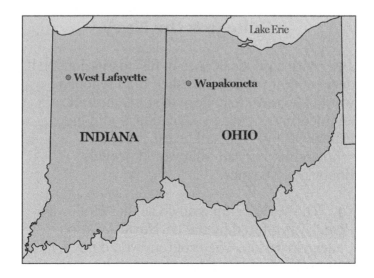

16. Neil started at Purdue University in 1947, just after his seventeenth birthday, but halfway through his second year he was informed that he would be joining the Navy earlier than planned. He was sent to the naval flight training school at Pensacola, Florida, where he would learn to fly fighter planes.

17. At Pensacola, Neil learned to fly the famous T-6 Texan, a single-engined training aircraft with a top speed of 210 miles per hour (335 kph). After a rocky start to his training Neil soon came to be regarded as a skilled and talented pilot.

The T-6 Texan

18. Neil graduated from flight training school in August 1950, and at the age of twenty he was a qualified naval pilot. He was due to go back to Purdue to continue his studies, but that plan changed when the United States went to war against North Korea. Neil was now sent to California where he joined Fighter Squadron 51 (VF-51).

19. VF-51 flew jet fighters, which Neil had never flown before, but he was soon impressing his fellow aviators, who held him in high regard, as a "fine young pilot...very serious and very dedicated."

20. Neil's squadron was assigned to the aircraft carrier "USS Essex", and it was on this ship that Neil and his fellow pilots learned an aviator's most difficult challenges - takeoffs and landings on an aircraft carrier.

USS Essex in 1951

21. An aircraft carrier has only about 500 feet (150 m) of runway space, which is bobbing up and down on the ocean. To make a safe landing a pilot has to catch a hook attached to the rear of his aircraft on one of four metal cables stretching across the ship's deck. The cable stops the speeding aircraft in just two seconds and prevents it falling over the end of the ship and into the water.

22. Neil made his first aircraft carrier landing on June 7, 1951, which he described as a "very emotional achievement." A few days later he was promoted to the rank of "ensign," and by the end of the month the USS Essex was sailing across the Pacific Ocean bound for the war in Korea.

Ensign Neil Armstrong

The Korean War

23. The Korean War began in June 1950, after the democratic country of South Korea was invaded by communist North Korea. America immediately went to South Korea's aid, while communist China and the Soviet Union sent soldiers to fight for North Korea. The war against communism was to last three years and claim millions of lives.

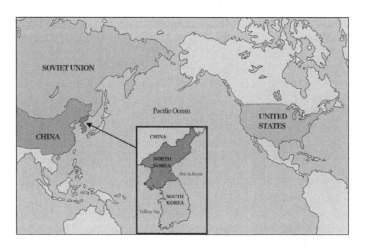

24. The job of Neil's squadron was to fly their jets from USS Essex to disrupt the enemy's transport system by bombing bridges and railroads. It was very dangerous as the planes had to fly very fast and very close to the ground.

25. Neil saw his first action over North Korea on August 29, 1951, when he flew a routine air patrol over the American naval fleet. Five days later Neil flew his seventh mission of the war - a mission that nearly cost him his life.

26. On September 3, while dropping bombs on a bridge in a hilly part of North Korea, Neil's low-flying Panther F9F jet hit a cable which the North Koreans had strung across the valley as a booby-trap. Six feet of the Panther's right wing was torn off.

Neil (in plane on left) in his Panther F9F

27. The plane was too badly damaged to be able to land, but Neil managed to fly back to friendly territory. His only option was to bail out using his ejector seat and parachute.

28. Neil flew his plane over the sea so that he could land in water and wait for Navy helicopters to rescue him. After ejecting from the plane he realized that he had misjudged the weather conditions and the wind blew his parachute back over land. He had a hard landing in a rice paddy field, but apart from a cracked tailbone he was unhurt.

29. Neil went on to fly a total of seventy-eight missions during the Korean War, and he returned home with numerous medals. He left the Navy in August 1952 to return to Purdue where he could continue his college education.

Test Pilot

30. Neil worked hard at Purdue and left in 1955 with a degree in aeronautical engineering. He also met eighteen-year-old fellow student Janet Shearon. They fell in love and became engaged a few months after Neil's graduation.

31. Neil's ambition was to become a test pilot. Not only would he be able to fly new types of aircraft, but he would also be involved in all aspects of aviation science and technology.

32. Neil had his heart set on working at Edwards Air Force Base in California, where cutting-edge testing on the newest and most revolutionary aircraft was taking place. It was there, just eight years earlier, that the legendary Chuck Yeager had become the first man to fly faster than the speed of sound. Neil wanted to be part of this exciting research.

Chuck Yeager

33. Unfortunately there were no openings at Edwards, but Neil found a test pilot post at Lewis Flight Propulsion Laboratory in Ohio. He spent a happy few months there before getting a letter from Edwards asking if he would like to transfer to California. Neil was being offered the job of his dreams!

34. Neil started work at Edwards in the summer of 1955, and a few months later he and Janet got married. They bought a run-down cabin high in the mountains that the newly-married couple slowly made inhabitable.

35. Neil and Janet wanted to start a family and in 1957 their first child, Eric, was born and two years later they had a little girl. Both children had nicknames - Eric was called "Rick," and Karen was known as "Muffie."

36. Neil flew all types of aircraft during his time at Edwards, but the most exciting was the X-15.

It was rocket propelled and could fly at a speed of nearly 4,000 miles per hour (6,400 kph). It could reach an altitude of more than 200,000 feet - nearly forty miles (65 km) high and at the very edge of space.

Neil and the X-15

37. In the summer of 1961, a tragedy struck the Armstrong family. Muffie, who was just two years old, had a fall and hit her head. She became very ill and doctors found an abnormal growth in her brain. There was no cure for the condition and Muffie died on January 28, 1962 - Neil and Janet's sixth wedding anniversary.

38. Neil was devastated by his daughter's death. He kept his sorrow to himself and didn't like to talk about it to anyone. He went back to work just a week after Muffie died.

39.   Neil spent seven years at Edwards, making over 900 flights and developing a reputation as a fine pilot and brilliant engineer. But early in 1962, he made a decision that would change his life - he applied to become an astronaut and become a part of the Space Race.

The Space Race

40. The Space Race began following the end of World War Two when the world's two superpowers - the USA and the Soviet Union - competed with each other to gain control of space and land a man on the Moon.

41. The first success of the Space Race was achieved by the Soviet Union on October 4, 1957, when an artificial satellite - Sputnik 1 - was sent into orbit around the Earth.

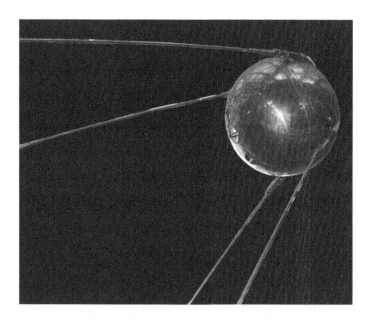

A replica of Sputnik 1

42. Two month's after the Sputnik launch, America responded with an attempt to send its own satellite into orbit. Millions of Americans watching the launch on live TV saw the rocket carrying the satellite explode as it tried to lift off. It was a humiliating failure for the United States.

The rocket explodes on the launch pad

43. The Soviet Union had more success on April 12, 1961, when the Soviet cosmonaut, Yuri Gagarin, became the first human being to reach space. His flight lasted 108 minutes as his Vostok spacecraft flew a complete orbit around the Earth.

44. Three weeks after Gagarin's flight, the United States responded by sending the first American, Alan Shepard, into space. His flight lasted just fifteen minutes and didn't reach Earth orbit, but it proved that America could at last compete with the Soviet Union.

Alan Shepard in space

45. Alan Shepard's flight convinced the American president, John F. Kennedy, that the United States could get to the Moon before the Soviets. He promised the American space agency, NASA, all the money it needed to land a man on the Moon before the end of the decade - just seven years away. It was a huge challenge for NASA.

President John F. Kennedy

46. In 1959, NASA had selected seven military test pilots from hundreds of applicants to train as astronauts on the new "Project Mercury." The "Original Seven," as they were known, were - Scott Carpenter, Gordon Cooper, John Glenn, Gus Grissom, Walter Schirra, Alan Shepard, and Deke Slayton.

The Original Seven

47. The aims of Project Mercury were to send a manned spacecraft into orbit around the Earth and to get it back safely, and also to see whether human beings were able to survive in the harsh environment of space.

48. The goal of sending a man into orbit was achieved on February 20, 1962, when John Glenn became the first American to orbit the

Earth. His five-hour mission was a complete success and the race to the Moon was on.

John Glenn

Becoming an Astronaut

49. In 1962, NASA decided to recruit more astronauts for the new "Project Gemini," which was to replace Project Mercury. Gemini would be even more ambitious than Mercury - it would test a human being's ability to live and work in space for long periods, and prove that it would be possible to send men to the Moon and return them safely to Earth.

50. Project Mercury and John Glen's historic flight excited Neil Armstrong, and although he preferred his aircraft to have wings, he decided to apply to NASA to become an astronaut on the new Project Gemini.

51. NASA had strict requirements for potential astronauts. They had to be experienced test pilots who could fly high-performance aircraft, under the age of thirty-five, and no taller than six feet. They also had to be college graduates with a degree in science or engineering. Neil fitted the bill perfectly.

52. Neil was just one of 253 pilots who sent their applications to NASA, but after sitting numerous written examinations and undergoing rigorous physical and psychological testing, he made it to the final thirty-two. From this group, in September 1962, nine men were chosen to be the next NASA astronauts - and Neil Armstrong was one of them!

53. The "New Nine," as the new astronauts were known, were unveiled to the American public in September 1962. Neil's fellow astronauts were Frank Borman, Charles Conrad, James Lovell, James McDivitt, Elliot See, Thomas Stafford, Edward White, and John Young.

The New Nine

Astronaut Training

54. Neil and his family moved from California to Houston, Texas, the home of the NASA Space Center. They were to live in a newly-built house at El Lago, a neighborhood they shared with other astronaut families and people working on the space program.

55. It was the beginning of a much happier time for Neil and Janet following the death of Muffie. Their son, Rick, was to get a brother when Janet gave birth to Mark in the spring of 1963.

56. The astronauts began a long, tough training period to prepare for surviving in space and undertaking the long journey to the Moon. The training was relentless, often lasting more than twelve hours a day, but Neil threw himself into it.

57. An important part of the training took part in simulators. The simulators gave an astronaut the feeling of actually flying in space and being in control of his spacecraft. Many procedures were being tried for the first time and the simulators allowed the astronauts to practice before having to carry them out in space.

58. To get used to the zero gravity that they would experience in space, the astronauts were taken on special flights in an airplane nicknamed the "Vomit Comet." A Boeing KC-135 would climb steeply into the air before plunging into a sharp dive. This created a few seconds of weightlessness during which the astronauts could float around inside the aircraft.

Mercury astronauts in the "Vomit Comet"

59. Not all the training was about flying spacecraft and surviving in space - the astronauts had to survive on Earth too. A spacecraft returning from the Moon could come down anywhere in the world if it was in trouble, and the astronauts needed to know how to survive in any environment until they could be rescued. One training expedition had Neil and a fellow astronaut left in a tropical rain forest for several days with just a tent and survival kit. They had to eat any bugs or roots they could get their hands on!

60. The parts of the training that Neil didn't enjoy that much were the public appearances. He had to spend a lot of time away from home, explaining to people the importance of the space program and why such enormous sums of money were needed for it.

Project Gemini

61.   After two years of training, the astronauts were ready to go into space as part of Project Gemini. Each Gemini spacecraft carried two astronauts, and they would spend up to fourteen days orbiting the Earth to test a man's ability to survive for long periods in space. Gemini was also used to practice the rendezvous and docking with another spacecraft - a procedure that would be important for a mission to the Moon.

62.   The first two Gemini missions were un-manned. "Gemini 3," the first manned mission, carried a two-man crew of Virgil "Gus" Grissom and John Young. Their flight lasted just under five hours and orbited the Earth three times. They succeeded in testing the new Gemini spacecraft in a near perfect mission.

63.   Gemini 4, the second manned Gemini mission, saw Ed White become the first American astronaut to perform a spacewalk. The twenty minutes he spent floating in space proved that a spacesuit could keep a man alive outside his spacecraft - which would need to happen when a man walked on the Moon.

Ed White during his space walk

64. There were three more Gemini missions before Neil got his chance as the command pilot of "Gemini 8." Its mission was to rendezvous and dock with another spacecraft already in orbit. It was the most complex and demanding mission so far.

65. On March 16, 1966, Neil and his co-pilot, David Scott, blasted off from Cape Canaveral, Florida, at the start of the Gemini 8 mission. Six minutes later they were orbiting 96 miles (155 km) above the Earth at a speed of more than 17,000 miles per hour (27,000 kph).

66. After three orbits of the Earth, Neil spotted "Agena" - the spacecraft that Gemini would dock with and that had been launched from Cape Canaveral earlier. After catching up with Agena Neil managed to successfully dock the two spacecraft, the first time the maneuver had ever been attempted.

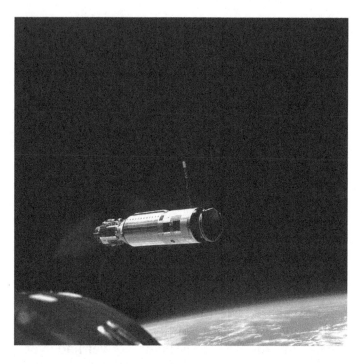

Agena seen from Gemini 8

67. Back on Earth there were cheers and celebrations at Mission Control, Houston, which was in constant radio contact with Gemini. But then Dave Scott sent a chilling message, saying – "We have a serious problem here. We're tumbling end over end."

68. Both spacecraft were spinning through space out of control. Neil made the decision to separate from Agena but it made no difference as Gemini continued to spin faster and faster.

69. Both astronauts' vision started to blur, and Neil knew he would have to do something quickly before they passed out. Using all his skill as a pilot and calling on the long hours of simulator training, Neil eventually managed to gain control of the Gemini spacecraft.

70. Although the two astronauts wanted to carry on with the mission, NASA insisted they return to Earth. So after just eleven hours in space, Gemini 8 headed home and splashed down safely in the Pacific Ocean.

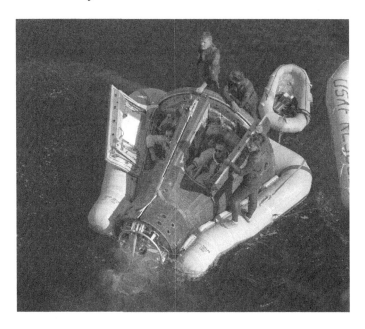

Gemini 8 shortly after splashdown

71. Neil was unhappy that he didn't complete the mission, and wondered if he had been responsible for losing control of the spacecraft. But the problem turned out to be with one of Gemini's thrusters, which are small rocket engines used to change direction.

72. Although the Gemini 8 mission nearly ended in disaster, NASA officials had been impressed with Neil's calmness and decision-making. This would be remembered when choosing astronauts for the future missions to the Moon.

73. Project Mercury and Project Gemini were both great successes, and proved that it should be possible to send a man to the Moon and return him safely to Earth. The Gemini missions were followed by the "Apollo Program," which would carry out even more testing and preparation in order to send men on the long journey to the Moon.

The Apollo Spacecraft

74.   Three spacecraft would be needed for a mission to land men on the Moon - a massive, powerful rocket would blast off into orbit above the Earth carrying two smaller spacecraft and a crew of three astronauts.

75.   Attached to the top of the giant rocket would be the second spacecraft - the Command/Service Module. The third spacecraft - the Lunar Module - would be packed in tightly behind and be pulled free and joined on to the Command/Service Module when in space. It would be the Lunar Module that would land two astronauts on the Moon.

Saturn V

76.   It would need an incredibly fast and powerful rocket to enable a crew of three astronauts and all their equipment to escape the Earth's gravity, so NASA engineers designed and built the biggest, heaviest, and most powerful rocket ever built - the Saturn V.

The Saturn V

77. The Saturn V rocket stood 363 feet (111 m) tall - as high as a thirty-six-story building. It was three times taller than the Gemini rockets and four times taller than the rockets used in Project Mercury.

78. The Saturn V was built in three sections - or "stages" - each filled with massive quantities of rocket fuel. When the fuel was used up in the first two stages, these would separate from the rest of the rocket and fall back to Earth. The third stage would be used to propel the Command/ Service Module towards the Moon, after which it would separate before traveling deeper into space and going into orbit around the Sun.

The Command/Service Module

79. The cone-shaped Command Module was where the astronauts lived and worked during the trip to the Moon, and connected to it was the Service Module which supplied the Command Module with rocket power, oxygen, and water.

The Command/Service Module

80. The Command Module was the nerve center of the journey to the Moon, and contained the instruments and controls which enabled the astronauts to fly the spacecraft on the right course. It was the only part of the Saturn V that returned to Earth under control - all the other parts either fell back to Earth, remained in space, or were left on the Moon.

81. When the time came to land on the Moon, one astronaut would remain in control of the Command Module as it orbited the Moon, while the other two astronauts would descend to the surface in the Lunar Module.

The Lunar Module

82. The Lunar Module was designed specifically for landing on the Moon. As there is no atmosphere on the Moon, the spacecraft didn't need to be streamlined or aerodynamic, and it looked unlike any other rocket ever built. Although it looked flimsy and fragile, it was a fine, robust spacecraft and was said to fly like a "nimble, responsive jet fighter."

The Lunar Module

83. The Lunar Module was built in two sections. The lower "Descent Stage" included the four long legs which would touch down on the Moon's surface, the engines to control the descent, and the fuel tanks.

84. The top half of the Lunar Module - the "Ascent Stage" - contained the crew's cabin and all the instruments and controls. When the mission was over the Ascent Stage would use its own engine to blast off from the Moon using the Descent Stage as a launch pad.

The Apollo Program

85. The first mission of the Apollo Program was due for launch in February 1967, but tragedy struck a month earlier when the crew lost their lives during a pre-flight test that went wrong. A fire swept through the Command Module killing astronauts Gus Grissom, Ed White, and Roger Chaffee.

Gus Grissom, Ed White, and Roger Chaffee

86. The Apollo 1 tragedy saw the Apollo Program pause for nearly a year as lessons were learned and changes made to ensure that nothing like that ever happened again. The Apollo 2 and the Apollo 3 missions were

canceled, and the program started again on
November 9, 1967, with the launch of Apollo 4.

87. Between January 1968 and May 1969, there
were six more Apollo missions. Each mission
built on the previous one, testing and perfecting
everything needed to pave the way for Apollo 11,
the mission which would finally see men walk on
the Moon.

88. The main accomplishments of the Apollo
missions before the launch of Apollo 11 were:

Apollo 4 - The first Saturn V launch (unmanned)
Apollo 5 - The first Lunar Module mission
            (unmanned)
Apollo 7 - The first manned launch of Saturn V
Apollo 8 - The first humans reach and orbit the
            Moon
Apollo 9 - The first manned flight of the Lunar
            Module
Apollo 10 - The Lunar Module descends to
            within nine miles (14.5 km) of the
            Moon's surface

The Earth seen from Apollo 8 during lunar orbit

Apollo 11 Astronauts

89.   In December 1968, while the Apollo 8 mission was taking place, Neil was told that he would command the Apollo 11 mission. He was also told that if Apollo 8 returned to Earth safely and there were no problems with 9 and 10, then Apollo 11 would be the mission to attempt the first Moon landing. Neil's fellow astronauts on the historic journey would be Edwin "Buzz" Aldrin and Michael Collins.

90.   Buzz Aldrin was a US Air Force pilot during the Korean War, and became an astronaut in 1963. He piloted Gemini 12 in 1966 when he set the record for spacewalks, spending a total of five and a half hours outside his spacecraft. He would become the second man to walk on the Moon.

Buzz Aldrin

91. Michael Collins had been a test pilot in the US Air Force. He joined NASA in 1963, and was part of the Gemini 10 mission in 1966, making two spacewalks. Collins would be Command Module Pilot and remain in lunar orbit while Armstrong and Aldrin walked on the Moon. His secret fear was that the Lunar Module's engine would fail to ignite when blasting off from the Moon, leaving Armstrong and Aldrin stranded.

Michael Collins

Launch Day

92. The launch of Apollo 11 was set for the morning of Wednesday, July 16, 1969, from NASA's launch complex at Cape Canaveral, where the Saturn V rocket was full of rocket fuel and waiting to blast off into space.

93. Four and a half hours before lift-off, Armstrong, Aldrin, and Collins had breakfast together before having a final medical check and being helped into the bulky spacesuits they would wear during the launch.

The pre-launch breakfast

94. At 6.30 a.m., three hours before the launch, the astronauts were driven to the launch pad where the Saturn V stood attached to the launch tower. An elevator took the three men to the top of the launch tower from where they could enter the spacecraft.

95. At 6.45 a.m. Neil Armstrong took his seat in the Command Module, followed by Collins and Aldrin. They carried out checks and procedures to make sure every part of the spacecraft was in order and ready for launch.

96. Shortly before 9.30 a.m. the final countdown began and the Saturn V engines burst into life. When they were at full power the rocket was released from the launch tower and rose into the air on a massive column of flames.

The launch of Apollo 11

97. The Saturn V accelerated to a tremendous speed - after just two and a half minutes it was moving at more than 6,000 miles per hour (9,650 kph), pushing the astronauts back into their seats and making them feel four times heavier than normal.

98. The rocket had been lifted into the air by the first stage, and when its fuel was used up, at an altitude of around forty-two miles (68 km), it was discarded and fell back to Earth. Stage two then took over, burning for around six minutes to take the rocket 114 miles (180 km) above the Earth. The speed reached 15,000 miles per hour (24,150 kph) before the second stage was discarded.

Apollo 11 at an altitude of thirty-nine miles, photographed from a US Air Force aircraft

99. The third stage burned for two minutes and took Apollo 11 into orbit, just twelve minutes after liftoff. The engine then shut down, and as they orbited the Earth, the crew carried out checks to make sure the spacecraft was ready to break free of the Earth's gravity and head for the Moon.

100. After one and a half orbits, the engine of the third stage was fired again. It burned for more than six minutes, providing "Trans-Lunar Injection," which increased the speed to 24,000 miles per hour (38,600 kph), pushing the spacecraft out of the Earth's orbit.

The Earth seen from Apollo 11 just after Trans-Lunar Injection

101. At just over three hours into the mission, the third stage was released and the Command/ Service Module was traveling under its own power. But the third stage still contained the Lunar Module which needed to be attached to the Command Module.

102. Four panels had opened in the third stage where the Lunar Module was stored. Collins, the Command Module Pilot, turned his spaceship around and headed to the Lunar Module where he could dock the two spacecraft. With the Lunar Module securely attached to the front of the Command Module, Collins turned around again and gave his engine a two-second burst which sent Apollo 11 on its journey to the Moon.

The Journey to the Moon

103. The astronauts spent the three days it took to reach the Moon making sure the spacecraft stayed in good working order, resting, and eating. They had been able to take off their heavy spacesuits and wore much more comfortable two-piece nylon jumpsuits.

104. Enough food and water for the eight-day mission had been packed on board the spaceship. NASA scientists had developed a nutritionally balanced menu of dehydrated and freeze-dried food, and the astronauts were able to enjoy meals such as beef stew and chicken soup.

105. The astronauts were in communication with Mission Control back on Earth for the whole journey. Michael Collins even slept with a small headset taped to his ear in case of emergencies, or if there were urgent messages that Mission Control might need to send.

106. People back on Earth were able to share in some of the astronauts' adventure. The crew made three TV broadcasts during the flight, showing millions of viewers dramatic images of the Earth from thousands of miles away in space.

***The Earth seen from Apollo 11 on day
three of the mission***

107. As Apollo 11 got further and further away
from the Earth the Moon's gravity pulled the
spaceship ever closer. At exactly the right time
Collins fired the engine to slow the spacecraft
down to a speed which would allow it to enter
the Moon's orbit.

108. As they orbited the Moon the astronauts
studied its surface, especially the intended
landing site on the Sea of Tranquility, chosen
because of its smooth, level surface. They then
settled down to sleep and prepare themselves for
the next day when Armstrong and Aldrin would
descend to the Moon's surface.

"The Eagle has Landed"

109. On the fifth day of the mission, Armstrong and Aldrin crawled down the connecting tunnel from the Command Module into the Lunar Module, which was known as "Eagle." Checks were carried out to make sure the spacecraft was good for undocking.

110. When the astronauts were satisfied, Collins pressed a button in the Command Module that separated the two spacecraft and Eagle floated into space under its own power. Armstrong radioed a message to Mission Control – "The Eagle has wings!"

The Lunar Module after separation

111. Armstrong and Aldrin fired the descent engine and Eagle began its journey towards the

Moon's surface. Collins would be left alone in the Command Module, orbiting the Moon for the next twenty-eight hours.

112. The descent proceeded smoothly apart from a moment of concern when an alarm light flashed on Eagle's instrument panel. Mission Control carried out checks back on Earth and decided that it was a false alarm and that the descent could continue.

113. As the landing site on the Sea of Tranquility came into view, Armstrong saw that it was not as flat as had been thought. The area was covered with large boulders and was not a safe place to land. Eagle was just 100 feet (30 m) above the surface and running out of fuel, but Armstrong managed to spot a place which would be suitable for landing.

114. With just seconds of fuel remaining, Armstrong guided Eagle towards the Moon's surface before landing safely in a cloud of dust. His heart rate had doubled to 150 beats per minute, but he calmly radioed back to Mission Control – "Tranquility Base here. The Eagle has landed!"

One Small Step

115.   It was planned that Armstrong and Aldrin would rest for four hours before heading out onto the Moon's surface. But both men were eager to walk on the Moon as soon as possible, so instead, they had something to eat before beginning the two-hour job of putting their spacesuits on.

116.   By now it was day six of the mission – Monday, July 21 - and 109 hours, 24 minutes, and 23 seconds after blasting off from the Earth, Neil Armstrong backed out of the spacecraft's hatch onto the ladder attached to one of Eagle's legs. When he reached the bottom rung he lowered himself onto the Moon's surface where he spoke the now famous words – "That's one small step for a man - one giant leap for mankind."

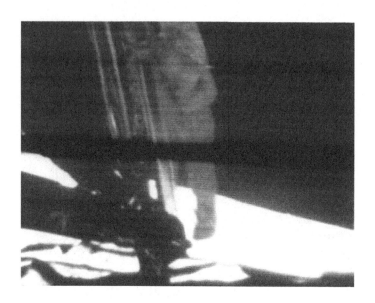

Armstrong descends the ladder

117. Armstrong's first job was to collect pieces of moon rock and soil, so that if there was an emergency and they had to leave in a hurry, at least scientists back on Earth would have samples of the Moon to study and analyze.

118. A few minutes later, Aldrin came down the Lunar Module's ladder to join Armstrong on the Moon. They then set up a TV camera so that people back on Earth could watch as they walked on the surface and set up important scientific experiments.

119. A "Laser Ranging Retro Reflector" was set up pointing back towards the Earth. It would pick up laser beams projected from Earth so that scientists could tell the exact distance between the Earth and the Moon. It would be accurate to within six inches (15 cm)!

120. A seismometer was set up to measure the strength of any "moonquakes" on the lunar surface. It was such a sensitive instrument that scientists back on Earth could detect the movement of the astronauts' footsteps!

Aldrin stands by the seismometer

121. A foil "flag" was unfurled to catch particles and gases reaching the Moon from the Sun. At the end of the moonwalk it would be rolled up and taken back to Earth for scientists to analyze.

122. Once the experiments were set up, the astronauts also unveiled a plaque attached to one of Eagle's legs. It read – "Here men from the planet Earth first set foot on the Moon, July 1969, AD. We came in peace for all mankind." They also planted a United States flag in the lunar surface and took a telephone call from the American president, Richard Nixon.

Aldrin salutes the US flag

123. After around two and a half hours on the Moon, Armstrong and Aldrin climbed back into the Lunar Module. They had been awake for twenty hours and needed rest before lifting off from the Moon to begin their journey back to Earth.

The Journey Home

124. When the time came to leave the Moon, many people at Mission Control were worried that the Lunar Module's engine wouldn't work, and the astronauts would be stranded for ever, unable to return to the Earth. But everything went perfectly as the Ascent Stage separated from the Descent Stage and headed for lunar orbit.

125. After six hours in orbit above the Moon, the Lunar Module docked with the Command Module, and Armstrong and Aldrin were reunited with Michael Collins. The Lunar Module was separated from the Command Module and drifted away before eventually crashing on the Moon's surface. Collins fired the Command Module's engine for two and a half minutes, accelerating the spacecraft out of lunar orbit to send the three astronauts on their journey back to the Earth.

Eagle approaches the Command Module

126. Two and a half days after leaving the Moon's orbit, Apollo 11 reached the top of the Earth's atmosphere. The Command Module was separated from the Service Module and turned so that the heat shield on its base was facing the Earth. The friction generated by speeding through the atmosphere would generate a temperature of around 5,000°F (2,760°C) and the heat shield would prevent the spaceship from burning up.

127. The Command Module hurtled towards the Earth at over 20,000 miles per hour (32,000 kph) - out of radio contact with Mission Control. Minutes later, at an altitude of 24,000 feet, two parachutes opened to slow the spacecraft down to a speed of around 120 miles per hour (190 kph) before the three main parachutes opened at 10,000 feet. The Command Module was now traveling at just over twenty miles per hour and splashed down gently into the Pacific Ocean.

128. Minutes after splashdown the hatch of the Command Module was opened by Navy frogmen, and the astronauts were winched into a helicopter and taken to the recovery ship, USS Hornet.

Navy frogmen reach the Command Module

129. As soon as they landed on USS Hornet Armstrong, Aldrin, and Collins were put in a quarantine facility to keep them out of contact with other people. Scientists were afraid that the astronauts could have brought dangerous organisms and bacteria back from the Moon.

***The astronauts in quarantine being
congratulated by President Richard
Nixon***

130. Armstrong, Aldrin, and Collins spent three
weeks in quarantine where they underwent
medical tests and checks. They were also able to
give NASA scientists and officials all the details
of their mission. They were finally released from
quarantine on August 10, 1969.

131. The astronauts were heroes to millions of
people from every part of the planet and they
spent the next two months traveling the world,

riding in parades, meeting world leaders, appearing on TV, and telling the story of their adventure.

A parade through New York City

Life after Apollo

132.   Neil Armstrong didn't much like the world-wide attention that being the first man to walk on the Moon brought. He felt that he was just a small part of the large team at NASA that made the Moon landing possible. He tried to live a quiet life, resigning from NASA and buying a farm in Ohio with Janet. He also became a professor of engineering at the University of Cincinnati.

133.   The fame and attention that Neil and Janet had to endure took its toll on their relationship. As a result, the couple sadly divorced in 1989, after thirty-eight years of marriage. Around the same time, Neil suffered a heart attack and lost both his parents.

134.   It was a bad time in Neil's life but everything changed in 1992 when he met Carol Knight, who was recently widowed and had two teenage children. Two years after their first meeting Neil and Carol were married.

135.   Neil remained busy giving speeches and making public appearances until his death on August 25, 2012, at the age of eighty-two, following complications after heart surgery. The US president Barack Obama led the tributes by saying, "Neil Armstrong was a hero not just of his time, but of all time."

136. Ten more astronauts walked on the surface of the Moon between 1969 and 1972, when the Apollo program ended. But it is the very first moonwalk that will be remembered as one of the greatest ever human achievements, and the name of Neil Armstrong will be remembered for a very long time.

For more in the Fascinating Facts For Kids series, please visit:

www.fascinatingfactsforkids.com

Illustration Attributions

A Ford Trimotor
Bzuk

The T-6 Texan
USAAF

USS Essex in 1951
U. S. Navy Bureau of Ships

Ensign Neil Armstrong
United States Navy

Neil (in plane on left) in his Panther F9F
John Moore, United States Navy

Chuck Yeager
U. S. Air Force

Neil and the X-15 : Alan Shepard in space : President John F. Kennedy : The Original Seven : John Glenn : The New Nine : Mercury astronauts in the "Vomit Comet" : Ed White during his spacewalk : Agena seen from Gemini 8 : Gemini 8 shortly after splashdown : The Saturn V : The Command/Service Module : The Lunar Module : Gus Grissom, Ed White and Roger Chaffee : Earth seen from Apollo 8 during lunar orbit : Buzz Aldrin : Michael Collins : The pre-launch breakfast : The launch of Apollo 11 : Apollo 11 at an altitude of 39 miles, photographed from a

U.S. Air Force aircraft : Earth seen from Apollo 11 just after Trans-Lunar Injection : Earth seen from Apollo 11 on day three of the mission : The Lunar Module after separation : Armstrong descends the ladder : Aldrin stands by the Seismometer : Aldrin salutes the U. S. flag : Eagle approaches the Command Module : Navy frogmen reach the Command Module : The astronauts in quarantine being congratulated by President Richard Nixon : A parade through New York City : Title page and final picture
NASA

A replica of Sputnik 1
NSSDC, NASA

The rocket explodes on the launch pad
U. S. Navy / NASA

Made in United States
Orlando, FL
18 January 2024

42653310R00046